When A Wolf Loves A Deer

Thomas Carlton

To those who are not afraid of love;
neither its valleys of pain, nor its summits of joy.

CONTENTS

ACKNOWLEDGMENTS

This book would not be possible without the support and encouragement of my family, Kim and Grady Moseley, The Aulettas, and the existence of a special woman: my friend, my love, my deer.

THE CHASE

It's a million year old game
primal
vicious in nature
yet at the same time
innocent.

Men chasing women
wolves chasing deer
lions chasing hyenas
in a never ending struggle born
of some necessary rhythm of the universe.
Sometimes it's bloody
sometimes it's violent
sometimes it's cruel
and yet other times it's as simple
and as honest
as a bottle of wine
two cups
summer stars
and a night walk along the harbor.

Don't let the surface fool you dear reader
for at the heart of this scenario
lies the same primal urge of the wolf
to chase
to catch
and to devour
the flesh and blood of the deer.
The man chases the woman
he strives to catch her
and like the wolf
he hopes to take her heart.

GLIMPSES

You exist, for me
as a collection of simple things
beautiful pieces of a larger puzzle
that I get quick glimpses of now and then
but never the full picture.

You're part of it
and so am I
and when I walk into your room full of sunshine
and fawn blonde hair
and I smell the hints of
coffee and sweat and flour that cling to you
and your pure brown eyes grab mine
and I feel the softness of your skin
the puzzle of the world
seems a bit more complete.

WINDOWS

They say one's eyes
are a window to their soul
well
your eyes are a door
to rich brown smooth hued worlds
of mermaids and volcanoes
and whales and turquoise turtles.

They look like Istanbul where the world was created.

I sail into them as a ship sails into open water
yearning and stretching
deck and canvas creaking
longing for the vast raging steel ocean
promising mystery chance adventure.

My heart quickens as it does
when strong gusts and salty swells
born hundreds of miles offshore
appear almost instantly.

My mind quiets as it does
when witnessing a sky teeming
with stars seen by a blessed few.

My body warms as it does
when washed clean
by pure consecutive
sunrises and sunsets.

I find myself hoping
they suck me in
and keep me.

LOVE IS A PINK SWEATER

It's pink and fluffy
it's soft and warm
it smells good.
It touches you in ways
normal things can't.

It's covered in fluff
and this is telling;
often times
the fluff ends up all over you
on your face
in your hair
under your shirt
stuck in your mouth.

The pink fluff has a mind of its own
it will appear when you least expect it
when you think you're impeccably cleaned up
dressed to the nines
the fluff sticks to your back
it can also catch the wind
floating away as you watch it go
powerless to get it back.

Perhaps a bird will use it for its nest.

Or you can pull a shirt out
that hasn't been worn for months
and the fluff will be there
pink
and laughing a bit
at its unexpected presence.

Love is a pink sweater
pink, fluffy, soft, warm
but mostly unpredictable and wild
like a piece of fluff in the wind.

DAY DREAMS

I find myself transported
to places I have never been
but they feel so real
so vivid
that I have no doubt they exist.

I find myself watching the sunrise over Saharan sand dunes;
the blood red rays cut through the dusty air
they illuminate the gossamer wings of locusts
as the sleeping camels at my feet slowly awake
to a new day.
Then I wake up
and the same sun warms the gold dunes of your hair
on the pillow next to me
and it is a new day
though without camels.

I find myself walking in humid jungles
chasing jaguars
being chased by Aztec warriors
Ayahuasca dream figures hanging from vines
applauding the chase.
I awake
and the jungle is replaced with paved streets
the jaguar is replaced by you
and the Aztec warriors
become the nameless faceless hundreds.

I find myself sitting
naked, cross legged, meditating
on the rooftop of the world
on nameless snow covered peaks
Himalayan spirits swirling on the wind
carrying Tibetan chants to my ears as the world waits

sleeping below.
I open my eyes
and there we are on your couch
you curled up in my lap
a warm sleeping cat
and my eyes still shining with snow and ice.

I wonder
if you know your role in all of this
or even if you're aware when I leave you
and when I come back
if you can see the places I have been
in my eyes.
No matter where you send me
regardless of the beauty or extravagance of the place
I am never upset when I come back
to you
beautiful you
because being with you
is the best dream of them all.

SOUL SEEING

To see a soul is to see the universe.
To hear a soul is to hear god.
To touch a soul is to touch the infinite.
To smell a soul is to smell the earth.

Your soul showed itself to me
as plainly as a flower shines in the sunlight
glistening with dew
perfection realized.
It did not reveal itself all at once
rather
the tiny cracks in your person
allowed it to shine through
and shine and shine and shine
until my eyes burned and watered.
I saw glimpses of vast grasslands littered with
dandelions, sunflowers, hyssop, sage, aster
all slightly swaying in a gentle wind.
Monarch butterflies, deer, chipmunks
and other peaceful creatures
played in the soft warm early morning sun.
The sky was azure blue
and giant clouds formed impossible shapes
and my eyes cannot stop looking.

Your soul echoed in my ear
as clear and as distinct
as the rush of wind through old-growth forest
or the moaning of a lonely mountain.
It took awhile to realize
in those calm, quiet moments
with my head pressed close to yours
that your soul was talking to me
comforting me with the language

of trees and mountains.
I hear it at night as I lay next to you
as sleep presses its weight upon me
and I feel as if I am enveloped
by the oldest forest
the tallest mountain
and I cannot stop listening.

Your soul touched me
as softly as a feather lands
gentle yet startling in its expansiveness.
I stretched out my open body on top of yours
slowly
like the tide that engulfs the beach
your soul engulfed me;
it felt as if I were submerged in a warm bath
your heartbeat was the only thing that I could hear
and it felt as if my physical body had dissolved
and your soul had become a container
for whatever remained.
I am not sure when it let me go
but I long for its touch still.

Your soul emanates a smell
that can only be described
as a summer night
a smell containing childhood memories
camping trips, trespassing, long walks in the dark
lightning bugs, thunderstorms, fireworks, crickets chirping
a train passing
long kisses and sweaty caresses.
I smell it after you take a shower
after you have washed the daily smells off of you
it wafts over me before I see you
when you enter a room behind me
I know that you are there
when I smell it

I press my nose into your skin
into the hair at the base of your neck
and I inhale
as if it were my last breath.

THE WOMAN

Every once in a while
a woman will shake you like a tempest
a freight train
a hundred hits of acid
a near life experience
a god sighting.

She will turn your brain
into a vessel designed for one thing
to see her in a light like no other.
Your eyes will notice new things
your mouth will taste new tastes
your skin will tingle in new ways
your heart will beat in strange rhythms
as the brain commands the whole body
in its new quest.

The eyes believe unbelievable sights.
Her hair is transformed
into living strands of silver and gold
that is haloed in light.
It glows in the night
as if it somehow retains the light of the previous day.
Her skin radiates the warmth of dawn's first rays
it warms you on cold nights, mornings
and even on nice days it feels warmer than the sun.
Her touch feels like lightning bolts on your skin;
you pull away
skin charred, hairs on end, gooseflesh.

Her body is alive.
Sea shells replace her fingernails
the hairs on her skin become like the soft belly fur of a tiger
her feet are alabaster smooth

her eyes, unblinking, huge, become magnetic orbs.
She wears Spanish moss across her breasts
and a ruby in her navel.
Where she walks
the ground is stained with love
and birds, cats, dogs, squirrels follow her footsteps.

They exist
rare
but there.
And if they leave you
you never quite recover
eyes scanning the ground for her footsteps
like the birds
the cats
the dogs
and the squirrels.

TOPAZ DOE

The Jade Buddha is no longer enough.
They should make intricate topaz figures
of a young beautiful doe lying in lush grass
a smile only the feminine mother can know
peaceful, innocent, fragile yet secure
emanating presence and love.

Even if the greatest sculptors
using the most precious topaz
worked ceaselessly for years carving such a figure
they would still fall short of capturing you.
They would miss the soft brown richness of your eyes
the way they look at a page, a bird, the trees.
They would miss the way your cheeks turn slightly pink sometimes
as if they somehow absorbed the excess heat of the room
so as to light up your eyes.
They would fail to capture the smell of a doe
the pureness of her heartbeat
the sound of blood running through her veins
the way in which even in a dark room
light follows her.

Most of all they would fail to express her immaterial beauty;
it can only be seen in person
in her smile
in her waking
in unexpected moments.
Such a figure could be given to me
worth its weight in gold
and I would choose a second with you
the real topaz doe
every time.

SAND CASTLES

Sun shining
can you see it
can you feel it on your skin
when the light catches in your eye
burning and sharp
leaving a white spot
of momentary blindness.

Waves whispering
mumbling in constant dialogue
with the shore and the sand
the short
loud exclamations as the waves hit
followed by
the long
slow hiss as they withdraw their previous statements
only to try
again and again
in a conversation that is eons old.

Sand shifting
the fine variety
white and light and almost annoying in its ability to cover every
surface
to traverse every barrier
to end up in your eyelashes or mouth or inside your ear
under your fingernails.
It painted her tan skin in intricate, delicate nature patterns
and when she moved
a blink of the eye, a shift of the head
it fell about her
and was replaced almost immediately
carried on the gusting wind
around under through our child's fort

made of shoes and tapestry and towel
and laying there just us two
all the while being covered in sand
and not a care in the world.

I could hear the sand tumble over the pages of your book.
I could hear it rattle around inside my ear as I leaned over and
kissed your salty lips
I felt it
tasted it in your mouth
and it was right and good.
When I pulled away
my nose left some sand on your cheek
my mouth some sand in your mouth
a communion.

Wind whipping
sporadic but stiff
enough to shake our fort to its foundations
to march armies of sand into our castle
to take her hair and make flying kite tails of it
whipping it to and fro
into her mouth her eyes.
The spirit of the beach
a spirit of change
of tides
of constant transformation
of living and dying creatures
crawled into our castle with the wind
and stayed
her shifting legs and body
so subtle so soft so much like the sea
it was like watching a hundred rising and falling tides
at once.

We made a castle

a sand castle for us to hide in
to shelter us from the wind and waves and eyes of others
to share our books and our hearts and our lips
and you were my sand queen
if only for a few hours
and maybe
I a sand king
but who knows.

I know I was close to you
our skin electric and hot in the summer spirit
not quite touching but still feeling the energy between us
and the small white hairs on your arms stood straight
as if electrified
and your smell overpowered even the beach smell
and I was as lost in it as a wolf would be in the city
I suppose.

I tried to read the words in the book before me
but my eyes could only read the lines in your hands
or the sand on your skin
or they would steal quick glances at your eyes
brown unlike mine
kind unlike mine
warm and inviting
unlike mine
like a cup of hot chocolate on a winter night.

Eventually, the sand won its assault
the spirit of the beach beckoned us to the ocean
so we left our castle
and like so many previous sand castles
it was destroyed by the rising tide.

TIME CRYSTALS

How rare it is
those nights
those days
those precious few moments
that crystallize in perfect clarity
so that the smells
the sounds
the quietness of the mind
the feeling of it all
is never forgotten and even on your deathbed
you are transported back
as if you were there again.

I remember still the night we walked along the harbor.
I remember many things from that night
the smells, the sounds
the tangible presence of desire and possibility
as thick as the humid summer air
both seemingly hell bent on drowning us.
But the way in which my body reacted to yours
has been burned into my memory
and I can only imagine
it is what being struck by lightning feels like.
Side by side
arms and legs bare
nothing but thick salty air between us
we walked by the sea.
It felt like my skin was trying to pull itself off of my
muscles, tendons, and bones
which held it prisoner in an effort to get closer to you;
it failed
and we continued walking as separate physical beings
close
but not too close.

I can still hear the sound of your voice
vibrating with new and beautiful notes
with ideas and beliefs
with promises unspoken
mixed with the unique blend of
waves, old trees, summer frogs, sleepy birds, city cats, southern
ghosts.
It is a soundtrack, a concert of our meeting
the first track of an album
I will no doubt wear out.

I can still recall sinking into a sliver of history
of night walks between men and women
on those old cobbled streets
the sea and the silent porches as witnesses.
Those aged oak trees and the dusty streets
have seen war and peace
love and hate
summers and winters
floods and earthquakes
and I was comforted as we walked among them
knowing that they smiled at our passing
our youth
the inevitable impermanence of all things
the powerful potential between us as we walked on.

And I can still feel the magnetic
gravitational desire to cross that barrier
which exists between two people
when their lives, minds, and bodies
are still entirely separate and distinct
as they have yet to make practical, mental, and physical
impressions on each other.
I wanted to reach out, to hold your hand
to kiss you, to stare into your eyes
to leave the first of many invisible marks on your body
with my hands and eyes, with my mouth.

I wanted to take out my brain
open it up like a trunk and show you my mind
lay out how I think
expose the thoughts
and beliefs
and ideas
that make me, me;
but that would ruin the process of exploration
the thrill of the battle of our minds
and what if it what you saw
scared you away?
No, no
I hid my mind from you
and worst of all
I remember losing a night
when I could have held your hand
kissed you
and stared into your eyes.

PORTALS

In that state of mind
He could have sworn
He saw her soul through her eyes.
For in that moment
she had no eyes
only huge pools of still midnight lake water
that sucked up all the stars and the moon
till even the infinite sky
that was never meant to be empty
was empty.

Those two orbs of beautiful brown
grew wider, larger, deeper
until they were big enough to walk through
which He did.

When such a thing happens
your soul comes racing out of your eyes like a man on fire
desperate to jump into the cool stillness
of that midnight lake.
His soul took a step
and another step
and then it walked out of His eyes
and then it ran.

He felt every step of His soul
as it traveled the distance to her eyes
there is no sound
there is no time.

Everything else disappeared
his mind stopped
and he waited in incredible anticipation.

His soul finally reached its beautiful brown home
and it rejoiced in the love it found there
for although it could not stay
it was enough to know
such a place existed.

RAINING

He felt like Michelangelo
Van Gogh
Picasso
Mozart
Magellan
as they stood awestruck
in the presence of the
Sistine Chapel
Starry Night
Guernica
The Magic Flute
the Spice Islands.

He felt like God on the seventh day.
He felt like a thief in the night
stealing glimpses of a beauty
he had no right to.

She stood there
naked
covered in a transparent gown of crystal raindrops.
She wore the pale
goldish light from the lone streetlamp
like a queen wears a crown
as if that color
that streetlamp
existed solely for her
as if it was her very skin
and the shadows from the trees
accentuated the shape of her calves
the curve of her breasts
the muscles of her back.

When she moved

the world moved with her
and when she stopped
so too the world.

He stood transfixed
like summiting a mountain
like seeing the night sky at sea
like watching the captivating savagery of nature.
It was a moment of such beauty
the naturalness of her skin meeting his
raindrops between them
that he would remember forever
and every time it rained
he thought of her face
laced with goldish drops of water.

FOOTPRINTS

You walk on my soul
leaving footprints as casually and as clearly
as if you were walking on the beach;
the footprints become memories I cherish forever
and are never erased by the rising tide of time.

The beach of my soul
windswept, without dunes, overwhelmed by violent tides
accepts your footprints with a hungry adoration
perhaps even reverence.
Like the lone beach walker
you rarely look behind you
and thus you fail to notice
the beautifully distinct pattern of footsteps
some deep and clear
others shallow and faint
that only you could create in that natural canvas.
I, however, have looked back
at the many marks you have made
and the first footprint is as utterly unique
as a piece of sea glass, a sharks tooth, or a broken shell.

It was a summer night
and like all summer nights in the South
it was hot, and humid;
but mostly it hinted at the exuberance of youthful spirit
of adventure.
I was sweating
not only because of the temperature
and the crowd of moving people
who frantically expressed that summer spirit
in time to the local band
but also because the ocean of my soul was raging
in a full moon high tide.

When I saw you
not for the first time
but in a way that instantly calmed the raging of the sea inside me
you stepped off the boardwalk
and that first footprint in the beach
was you entering the story of my soul.

We sat not far apart
you across from me at a narrow table
and I drank your image
more quickly than the drink in front of me.
I waited more impatiently
for the passing of your gaze
than for the rare gusts of cool wind
and you sparked the insatiable hunger
for the sound of your voice
which I battled to hear over the music.
You told me of a trip you were about to depart for
and you laughed in a casual way
as if you were going no farther than across the street
but the light of adventure shone in your eye
and your smile said that you were ready
that you were always ready
and I fell in love with your smile
right there at that table.

The minutes passed
both of us talked sparingly
yet I was intrigued by the depth hidden in your eyes
and the potential behind your words.
Music surrounded us
as did the summer drunk atmosphere
and I felt the slowing of time
which happens when your focus sharpens to one point.

I wonder if you were aware

that I watched you as a wolf watches its prey
or a painter studies its subject;
if you could feel the intensity of my focus on your skin
on the wetness of your lips
on the sweat cooling on your chest;
if you knew that I was memorizing how you sat
how the wind played with your hair
how you smoked your cigarette.

You were busy making
the first of many footprints on my soul
and if I am honest
neither of us knew it then.
When we said goodbye
something that would become a painful habit for us
and although it was easier then than it is now
I still felt a shadow of the sadness and longing
that I feel at every parting.

NIGHT AND DAY

For what is the sun without the moon?
His burning, raging, fiery intensity
like the sun
found its match
in her moon like cool, calm consistency.

Or the night sky without the stars?
His capacity for darkness
subtle yet strong
found its equilibrium
in her everlasting light.

They were as different as fire and water
but what is the light without the dark?
The mountain without the valley?
The ocean without the shore?

Like all natural polarities
they knew that one existed in the other;
the light in her eyes was his light reflected back to him
just as the moon mirrors the sun;
the fire on his skin was her energy
coursing through the space between them.

And like the sun and the moon
they chased each other
across space and time
in a delicate dance
that left them yearning
for more
more
more…

LEAVINGS

The pain of leavings
of goodbyes
of breaking those last precious seconds of eye contact
knowing it may be weeks or months
until the warmth of that soul touches you again
feels like a cat jumping on your heart
twenty pounds of weighted fur falling from a great height
yet making only the slightest thump when it lands.

Or the sound a record player makes
after the record is over
spinning white noise
so abrupt
after the beautiful notes have ceased playing.
It's the one cloud
on a perfectly sunny day
that suddenly throws you in shadow
and without thinking
you glance up at the sky
expecting a thunderstorm to have crept out of nowhere.

That is how I feel when I leave you.
It is as if my heart tapes a little piece of string
to yours
and when I have to walk away from you
the string keeps us together
until a car door
or simply too much distance
breaks it in half.
Then I walk along
dragging my half of the string
on the ground behind me
waiting for the moment when
I can reattach it to yours.

JAIL HOUSE DREAMS

A plane might as well be a five star hotel
in comparison to jail.
I swear it is designed with the intention to prolong suffering
that some devil
in some gloomy city office
sat down with pencil and paper
and began with great zeal
the task of creating the most miserable collection
of right angles
and flat surfaces possible.
The huge, glaring, spiteful iridescent lights
hang above you like the lights of the surgeon's table
blinding and hot and irritating
they hide scalpels and machines of pain
and masked fiends
who are preparing to cut you open.

There are no nights in jail
just endless hours of hot white light
that drag on into eternity
and your eyes begin to thirst for the dark
because even when you close your eyes
that damn light seeps in
reminding you where you are.

The white painted cinder blocks feel heavy around you
giving the impression that you're underground
and a mile of dirt separates you from freedom.
They trap a bone chilling cold all around you
so that you wear it like a cloak of ice
shivering in thin, striped jumpers.
Oddly enough
the chairs are those hard plastic models
found in schools

and lunch comes in brown paper bags;
it's all so seemingly innocent
like school
but the teachers are replaced with guards
and the only lesson to learn
is the value of freedom.

The cells that lined the walls
provided some measure of security
in their quietness
in their isolation
from the other blank faced, cold, bored humans
who had committed unknown horrors.
I laid in C9 for hours
tossing and turning on the cold metal slab cot
until my thoughts began echoing off the walls
and I had the urge to talk to myself.

So I began pacing
up and down
up and down
to the latrine and back to the door
over and over
like some caged wolf
who hears the wild call to him at night
as the moon whispers down to him
promises of endless pristine woods and warm running deer.
A guard told me to sit down
to stop moving.
I stopped living
for I forget how many hours.
My sedated brain lied to me
painting pictures of death
infinities of imprisonment
and when it wasn't lying it was as silent as the grave
a blank slate, an organism in distress
which had shut down in self-preservation.

My body was dragging ball and chain
bruised ribs throbbing
muscles dead tired from fighting eight
or nine ER nurses in a battle of desperation
that they couldn't understand
wrists bruised from too tight restraints and handcuffs
hands dirtied
eyes blank as slate.
I was too far-gone to feel relieved
to feel anything when I was released in my hospital scrubs
as if straight from the insanity ward
and me being in that state of mind
lying on a bench and waiting
just waiting
mind off
for someone or something to rescue me.

Me falling asleep
sock feet hanging off the end of the bench
dirty hands over eyes
tangled hair everywhere
dreaming of hell and dripping ceilings and fire
even though I was impossibly cold;
and then I heard your voice as if from a long ways off
and through a dense fog
and I was sure I was hallucinating
for how could you
beautiful you
exist in such an ugly place
but the sound grew stronger
and I knew then that it was you
and I was filled with joy
as sudden as the eye of a hurricane
and I raised my head
and there you were
your back to me
but unmistakably you
with your waves of golden hair

lighting up that steel grey place
and already your presence transforming
the oppressive weight atop of me
into lightness.

I approached you from behind
you unaware
and I waiting to see your face
to see in your face and in your eye
a hint of forgiveness
and to know that you were safe
and I was afraid with each closing step
to be struck swiftly down by blame and hate.
With bated breath I reached out to your shoulder
just as you turned around
and what I needed sat there quietly
in your dimples
in your eyes
in the unbelievable smile
that swept the shards of glass from my mind
tore down the walls around my heart
and shattered the shackle around my ankle.

Thomas Carlton

TRIBUTE TO THE TREES

You stood there
so tall
so strong
so quiet
supporting our frail frames
in the twists and bends of your natural shapes;
shapes only nature can produce
shapes that we sat in, laid in
and stood in.

You watched us with kind eyes
eyes devoid of judgment
eyes full of compassion as we played in your home.
You watched us as you would a bird or a squirrel
even though we lack their innocence.
You watched as we kissed fifteen feet above the ground
safe in your arms, saved from judgment
and the vicious eyes of others
by your blanket of leaves.
You kissed the sun
the air
the dirt
much more grateful for the world around you.

You shared with us
shivered as we touched each other's faces
as we held onto your trunk
letting our bodies come together.
You shared the secrets of the world with us
that the silence everyone is looking for
exists in the tops of the trees
where only children can find it
even if we were to forget it
as soon as we left your branches.

MUSE

You are the source
the inspiration
the spark igniting 10,000 gallons of gasoline
into an inferno of desire
a super nova of inspiration
a torrential downpour of creativity
that washes the dust of fruitlessness
and impotence from my bones.

You are a window to the infinite beyond both of us
but you are also a mirror reflecting the infinite back to me
and a speaker playing the still notes of silence
that is the source of all creation
and a magnifying glass that focuses the light of freedom
until it burns a hole in my flesh.

I enter your presence
like walking across the threshold of the chapel
like entering the deepest darkest forest
like taking a breath of air before the dive
like drifting into sleep.
My brain performs libations
my heart conducts ablutions
my soul is baptized
my skin confesses wordlessly
my eyes chant at the sight of you.

I leave your presence
like a child leaves the womb
like a baby bird leaves the nest
like a monk leaves the monastery
like a fish leaves the water;
I instantly desire to return to you
to return home

to feel the cleansing waters wash my bones clean
to feel the burning light on my flesh
to see through you.

I crave your skin
your hair
your smile.
Lost and uninspired
I wander the streets
looking through meaningless windows and dull mirrors.
I thirst to hear your voice
the sweet melody of your laugh
the gentleness of your words.
I want to drink your voice
like the alcoholic wants to drink his whiskey.
Parched
I prowl the bars in search of some respite
but never find any.

I hunger for your sweet mouth
your dimples
your soft places
the lush ravines of your neck
your soul.
I want to devour you
to absorb the sun essence trapped in your eyes
to eat the infinite oceans of love in your lashes
to taste your dimples filled with lakes of creativity
and so I hunt tirelessly for you
sniffing the air for a hint of your smell
stalking the ground for a trace of your step
listening intently for the still notes of silence
like a starving wolf.

SPRING

She came
and went like a summer rainstorm
too fast
to make the hard packed earth
scarred with tiny ridges of mud and dust
soft and open to the sun again.

She came
and went softly
with grace
and she left her scent subtly on the sheets
as unique and unmistakable
as the first swift showers of spring
with their pure clean promises of growth and sun.

She came
and went
and the dogwoods sat and watched
wagging their tails
smiling that dog smile
because they were happy that she was on their street.
The witch-hazel stained the air with its approval
as she walked by
and the full moon beamed a clear path for her
and the sun was jealous that he could not share
in that moment.

She came
and went
and I lay there in the sheets
like a budding flower in the damp spring earth
greedily soaking up what she left behind
as a blue jay sang its happy spring song
at my window.

JOURNEY

When I am with you
I am transported to other worlds
I close my eyes
and my mind creates new planets in your freckles
and star systems in your beauty marks
and hidden treasures within the soft swirls
of your brown skin.

I enter lush green valleys in the dip of your neck
tasting banquets of the richest foods
as my mouth travels
from the soft holes in your collarbone up to your face.
I dive into azure oceans of pristine water when my mouth finds
yours;
I am lost within it
as is a whale in its home.
I walk through ancient prairies as I get to your hair
untouched by man
golden grass blowing in the wind
carrying the smells of promises of tomorrow.
I climb peaks
for your breasts are summits I never tire of climbing.
When I descend
I lay down on your thighs
in cool beaches of the softest sand
and the racing of your heart
sounds like the murmuring of waves.

My hands become explorers of undiscovered paradises
as they travel over your body;
my eyes become camera lenses
as they capture and store every detail
the triangle of freckles on your left arm
the crease of the soft dimples on your cheeks

the arch of your foot
the blush like a sunset on your chest.
You are the unexplored wild
full of unexpected secrets and danger
gentle and savage;
my blood boils
my mind races
at every opportunity to enter your wilderness.

KANSAS

I wait in great expectation
for the swelling of spirit
the broadening of horizons
the expansion of my universe
which occurs at the simplest moments;
the touch of our foreheads
sunlight trapped in your eyes
an innocent hello.
It feels like the ferocious inhale of air around an inferno
as urgent and desperate
as a drowning man clawing for air.
Or standing in the middle
of endless Kansas
surrounded by infinite miles of grass
and overwhelming empty space
where you feel a simultaneous increase
and decrease of all things possible.
You stand there
ignorant of your power
unaware of the raging tempest you create in me
and it's all the more beautiful
that way.

SEASONS OF THE HEART

Like the summer when we first began
you started hot and strong;
your love made me sweat
I could hear your voice in the cricket's song
see your face in the raging sun
feel your cool touch on my sun red skin
smell you in the burnt grass.

I suppose you were simply following the seasons
and why should I be surprised
that when the days became colder
the nights longer
so too
did you.

I watched the leaves turn from green
to yellow
to blood red
then drop to the ground
to be reduced to dust
under the passage of time
and the heels of strangers.

Then winter came upon me;
your absence left me cold and shivering.
I couldn't hear your voice
and it was as if a deep blanket of snow had fallen
cutting off all trace of your existence
the winter grey sky hid your face
and I was left only with the smell
of the uncaring ice around me.

LIGHTNING

The beach welcomed us with an open heart.
The moon smiled knowingly of the things to come.
The sea caressed our feet and ankles in her cool hands.
The sky showed us our short
beautiful
violent lives in a mesmerizing display of lightning
thirty miles out to sea.

I could see her face in the clouds
illuminated by glittering lightning
turned pink, her cheeks
in short flashes of
white light, her smile.
I could feel her hair in the wind surround me
like a warm protective blanket.
I could smell her scent
ozone and beauty
in the lightning.
I could hear her laugh
rumbling and dangerous
in the thunder
and I knew
somewhere far away
the mountains howled her name.

Oh
how I howled back in vain
lips closed
head thrown back
eyes wild with doubt
in a hidden struggle as vicious
as a pack of wolves
even as she stood six feet next to me
her golden hair glowing in the moonlight

close enough to disappear
far enough to reach
caught in a place
where I longed to meet her
but couldn't.

So I ran
up and down the shore
to the mountains and back
in an endless race against
her name echoing in the valleys
her laugh in the thunder
her scent in the lightning
her hair in the wind
her face in the clouds.

I was exhausted
I stopped running
I sat
I waited.

SORRY

I guess it happened gradually
you were there from the beginning
before the chaos and pain
and I wonder if you noticed the shift
if my eyes betrayed me
so that you could see the weight of it all
or if I hid it so well
maybe even from myself
that I would have to explain it to you.

I began to gravitate towards pain
like helpless moths fluttering toward a fiery death
in iridescent coffins
until pleasure became uncomfortable
and I transformed even the most beautiful moments
into a bed of hot coals to walk across on the way to joy.

I began to be content with being lost
like those geese that never make it south in winter
and end up in grimy backyard pools
or public parks
or private manicured lawns
dodging pissed off landscapers
never reaching the warm golden shores of Mexico.

And I began to embrace fear
like a wild animal that has its leg stuck
in the jaws of a steel trap
and the wind and trees and shadows
that were once comforting and home
have become dangerous and foreign
and even the smallest sound or movement hints at danger.

I never intended to become this way
so removed from the wild freedom of a strong spirit
that we are all born with
but I have become
and I am not fit to be in your presence;
my words
and tears
and blood
I spill in a futile apology to you
but you remain
and that I cannot explain.

WAITING

If only you knew the depths of my intentions
the subversive motives behind every kiss
and every letter
and every glance
sent in your direction.

Perhaps
instead of smiling in appreciation
instead of accepting these gifts
you would shudder in horror in the new understanding
that for every kiss I have given
I sought to forever mark your lips
with my name
with my memory
with pain and pleasure.

I strove to tattoo your skin
with permanent bites and long, red lines
from the passion trapped in my mouth and hands.
I hoped to forever stain you with my smell
so that if anyone else got close enough
they would sense that I was there
somehow.

I tried to burn the image of my face
and naked body onto the surface of your eyes
so that if anyone looked into them
they would see me.

If that were true
perhaps I could understand
why the kisses slide off your lips
why the letters end up crumpled and discarded

why the glances I put so much energy into are ignored
why the marks I leave on your skin fade
and are hidden
why your eyes resemble blank slate.

But it is not true
the motives I have are honest
and my love is pure;
so I stand in awe at the futility of my actions
waiting
waiting
waiting to leave a mark.

SNOWFLAKE

I never saw you for what you were
not because
of any deception
but because
I saw what you are.

I didn't hear
the beating of your heart;
I heard the eruption of a volcano
and the quietness of space.
I didn't hear
the words formed by your mouth
oh that wonderful mouth
where the answers to all the questions I had, hid;
I heard the sound of silence
the melody of the wind.

I didn't see
the rise and fall of your chest as you lay next to me;
I saw a high tide
and a low tide.
I didn't see
the opening and closing of your eyes;
I saw the sun rise
and the sun set.

I didn't see
the indifference in all your actions as you;
I saw a snowflake floating in the wind
and when you finally landed in my open hands
you melted on contact
with the intensity of my actions
with the heat of my passion
and I lost you forever.

LOVE LOST

I'm sorry
I gave you everything I had
and couldn't consider that you didn't want it
now I feel empty
like a charred, smoking
still warm firework casing
laying on the sidewalk after the 4th of July
my brothers and sisters in similar condition
strewn around me.

Just seconds earlier
we sprayed our insides into the night sky
lighting up the eyes of the youthful and elderly
with memories of summer nights
cold ice cream warm breezes soft kisses
hard bites moist grass dim lightning bugs
strong laughs weak fights
red white and blue.

Like a firework
whose sole purpose is to amuse for four seconds
I hope my efforts
were not in vain.

FAREWELL

I will watch you from afar
you who were once my shining star
like an unwanted lover waits in the night
remembering how we were so bright
here but never more to stay
I finally found the words
you wouldn't say.

ABOUT THE AUTHOR

When A Wolf Loves A Deer is the first published work by Thomas Carlton, a native of North Carolina. An early exposure to literature and the great outdoors cultivated a passion to express his intertwining's with the natural world. He studied religion at the College of Charleston and all things spiritual draw his attention. In other respects, he is a fearless lover, an avid adventurer, and a loyal friend. He currently resides in New York City where he is pursuing too many avenues to list. The author can be reached at pan.press.usa@gmail.com.

www.ingramcontent.com/pod-product-compliance
Lightning Source LLC
Chambersburg PA
CBHW021145020426
42331CB00005B/909